The Ohio State University Press/*The Journal Award* in Poetry

FAIR COPY

Rebecca Hazelton

THE OHIO STATE UNIVERSITY PRESS | COLUMBUS

Library of Congress Cataloging-in-Publication Data
Hazelton, Rebecca, 1978–
 Fair copy / Rebecca Hazelton.
    p. cm. — (Ohio State University Press/The journal award in poetry)
  "All poem titles are Emily Dickinson first lines, and each poem is an acrostic of that line."
  ISBN 978-0-8142-5185-0 (pbk. : alk. paper) — ISBN 0-8142-5185-4 (pbk. : alk. paper) —
 ISBN 978-0-8142-9302-7 (cd)
  1. American poetry—21st century. I. Title. II. Series: Ohio State University Press/The
 journal award in poetry.
  PS3608.A9884F35 2012
  811'.6—dc23
                        2012015273

Paper (ISBN 978-0-8142-5185-0)
CD-ROM (ISBN 978-0-8142-9302-7)

Cover design by Mia Risberg
Type set in Adobe Janson
Printed by BookMobile

9 8 7 6 5 4 3 2 1

Contents

3. THE GLOW OF THE BIG CORRECTION

Acknowledgments

All poem titles are Emily Dickinson first lines, and each poem is an acrostic of that line.

Poems from this manuscript have appeared in the following journals: *Pleiades, FIELD, The Sycamore Review, The Journal, Web Conjunctions, GulfStream, Drunken Boat, The Notre Dame Review, Nimrod,* and *Verse Wisconsin.*

Thanks to Frank Giampietro and Sandra Simonds, David Kirby, and Andrew Epstein for their valuable feedback.

Finally, I'd like to thank my husband, Mark Stafford.

[*Were it but Me that gained the Height*—]

World like a coat, silver clasps,
      ermine lined, warm with the dead inside,
rolling around in the red center—I thought

everything had a purpose—this was back when
      I still drank—and wasn't I a special
traveler, nestled in that pocket amongst the

butterscotch candies, the matchbooks?
      Unessential but accounted for, a steady
thing to touch. World like a

morning glory, withered every
      evening, world like a bristling dog,
terrified of thunder—I can't believe

how I believed, or how that belief
      assumed a shape around my body,
taking on the imprint of my heat,

gaining solidity. When
      anyone questioned me, I held
it forth, let them touch the sleeve—I

needed nothing. World like an
      egret, still and white on the highway
divider, world like a regret

typed out and then erased—I cannot
      hold you any closer without
everyone seeing, I cannot

hold you at all, it seems, your
      evergreens, your curling potato vine;
it's all too much much, and I a bit of

goosedown, a thistle fluff, naked and
		hatless, unaccounted for and extra,
the world like a world like a world.

1. ALL THAT I LOVE, I TREMBLE BY

[Summer laid her simple Hat—]

Sand dunes, lined with scruff. Please walk not
        upon their pristine, says the post. Also,

may you not swim in the red flag's warning,
may you observe proper safety, as there is no
        Eagle Scout on duty.

Regarding that nostalgia you smell: it's only burning scrap,
left unattended by teenaged boys who
are as fierce as the gulls that scuffle
        in the idiom of the Furies, and both
dive into the ocean like knives, both
           hover above what they covet.

Ecru is the color of my true love's sand, cerulean his
        regular sky. Beige on beige my echo,
scraps sending prayer smoke beige to the sky.

I loved a boy who burned
my body, left me an echo calling and calling.

Please respect the slumping bodies
laced with scruff. Walk not upon their forms.

        Echoes of summers of summers,
hot sand that made me skip like
a flat stone thrown from a boy's hand, that dashes
then drops out of sight.

[I gave myself to Him—]

I thought it something small. Everything was.
   Girling from one party to another—I was the prettiest
abbess, my wimple crisply folded, my cocktail habit
     vaccinating me against all thought. *Amor vincit omnia*
        engraved the length of my thigh,
        my pictures all black-barred.
Yes, I was a yes girl. Yes, I had such fun I can't
    say I remember. But gradually a heresy took hold—
et tu, Brutal, broke across the horizon
      like a hand snuffing out the sun.
For all your cruelties, you're the Him
       that I write to, letter after letter, requesting
only that you return me to my prior state.
       Have pity on a girl of Catholic tastes.
I want the same as anyone, just more, and faster.
Make nice, make haste, I say, and never yield.

[*At last, to be identified!*]

A dirigible powered us through the first leg,
      traversing snow-capped mountains where goats
leapt from crags, and men with wrinkled
      apples faces looked up, pointed.

Smiling
      to cold air, I slept under a bear skin,
         touched your lips in the night.

      On our pleasant soap
bubble journey, we dropped baskets down
      each morning, hooked meats, cheeses;
      in later weeks, nothing. Still, we took notes,

detailing the weather conditions, the migrating
      elk numbers and their steady decrease.
Northward by cracked compass,
      the sleet sheeting the balloon drove us low, then lower—

In time we cut through the ice, sank
fathoms into the sea, chaperoned by seals
      that are not mermaids at all.

Else you think this a hoax, know my hand—
down here still—please send help.

[Afraid! Of whom am I afraid?]

All that I love, I tremble by—all that pleasures
      for a moment brings regret by morning,

remembrance is to rosemary as rue is to forever—
A little birdie told me he no longer loved me.
           I plucked its
           downy feathers; I split its skin
           open. My hands still glow
        from the morning after
        what I can't remember—

How this holler in its breast shows me
      of the drowning set, how this
moment is recorded in the spine.

      A gold *no* spelled against the viscera;
my love wrote it there for me.

          I know this organ by its gravity—
            and borrowed
          feathers can't disguise how his eyes
       retreat from mine—

and the dull light I emit in the dark
isn't enough to read this heart, to parse the worms that nibble
      destiny, the word we use for *doomed.*

[*Delayed till she had ceased to know*]

Deluge against my attic roof
        evokes the flood and fickle God
laying waste to his invention—reminds me how

as a creature, I pair; I tandem to
        your side, happy in our sameness—
                else one more unmatched creature,
                drowning.

                The front yard
                    is churned red muck, rivulets—

last night, I told you *the car is stuck, and so am I*—no, not
                last night—long ago, it was

summer, it stormed every afternoon, and the pages
        hustled to my hand, promising answers—

even when I folded them into doves, released them over the waters—
                                    nothing
        hastened me to land.

All lags; the tiny boat perches on a hill,
        delayed. It will unfold and all creation

collapse out in a long giraffe,
emu, otter, gnu. I've wished that ark door wedged shut,
        and all earth's progeny left waiting
such as I've been.
Even the skittish know more bliss than I, and faster.

Doubtless as the sea, doubtless as this seeming,
the boat is so small I might pluck it loose from the land,
or tip the ocean in.
Know me as a new god,
neither angry nor ruthlessly hygienic.
Only lonely in this bathtub,
water all around.

[*A darting fear—a pomp—a tear—*]

Awake—and fear sits on my chest, a soot cat
dipping a crumbling black paw in my mouth. This is not the air
advertised, the dawn applied for. Yesterday was nice.
      Really. I walked on my feet like a dolly. I ate seven seeds

to every pomegranate. Curled and coiffed. Coiled and cuffed.
Inside the stiff fold of my Windsor knot, I hid my master's
      note: *Come live with me and be my love.*
      Go home straight from work—that H a hook
fixed deep in my cheek. I was this body,

except burning happy,
arrayed a radiant dandy, mustache waxed, waistcoat
right sharp. Now, I drink the champagne
      alone, watch QVC for hours, my phone impiously silent.

Possibly these tears are mine.

On the couch, I fumble to orgasm, sink beneath the cushions, the
                                    baseboards,
meeting no resistance through igneous, through
pillowy lava, and there to rest,
a molten golden baby in the earth's hot belly.

There I am, still. It's the body above that's a lie.
Eating, defecating, allowing fear to lap up
      all the air in the room. I hate how it wears my face
remembering the house where we were to live.

[A Sickness of this World it most occasions]

And in the blue dawn, that prickling
      sensation around the neck—as if
I've forgotten something—but everything is
      counted and placed. The stove is off,
          kitchen unlit.
Nothing here
emits light, all reflects reflected
          seeming—the idea of a thing but
slightly less. It's not so bad.
Only a feeling, only a foreboding, a
          feeling is only

      the moment before we've
had it, then missed it.
It's flavored like a
song you heard, too young to understand,
      wanting to crawl between the notes,
onto the singer's soft throat thrumming,
         right to the part where
love happens. It's a sickness,
             desire.

In the room too hot to make love,
the fan wobbles—
make love—whoever thought I'd say that
of chemical imperative—but there is
something
      that lingers
outside the bedroom where

chickadees are mimicked by mockingbirds, and
crow feathers hold color in their grooves like
      an old LP—the needle lowers to my
sacrum, to my nape, and myself a spiral—

in the morning's noise, I spin
       out a song I'm forgetting,
no, that you have, what
shouldn't be missed, but is, but was.

[*The nearest Dream recedes—unrealized—*]

Then we set up a sort of camp beneath the sea,
hung shells stuffed with phosphorous plankton,

emitting a cool green light—by which to read.
Nothing from the radio, and we stopped listening

eventually, finding it was easier to forget
a world above—it seemed almost laughable!—than

remember we were ourselves forgotten.
Eating was not difficult. The giant fish, blind

seekers, nuzzled up to us and we speared
them in their dumb trust. Their flesh was

dense, webbed with fat. We were warm
regardless of the ocean's chill, wrapped in an

excess of food and salt. Like teenagers,
arms and legs sprawled on the sea floor.

My dreams were small boats sailing,
rigged with high-tension spider silk,

eels nosing the hull to push us further.
Catching sight of land, we'd descend, dry

eyed and sober, to meet the feathered
denizens of this new world. Such

ego, you'd tell me in the waking, a continent
so mapped for my pleasure, rivers following

unquestioning my hand. But they are mine,
notwithstanding your presence, and such dreams

relax into memory, given time and a pinhole's
eke of light. We need so little to develop

a clear picture. You try to signal
lightweight planes that X our island, but no one

is transmitting the coordinates of our smoking
zeppelin, or sees the fiery words we've spelled with

each grain of molten sand. I want us undiscovered,
damned to this partnership, to each other.

[*Let my first Knowing be of thee*]

Lest there be confusion, understand: only
  envy of your tabula rasa
    tongue
    made me doubt
    your sincerity, not your quiet
footsteps across the oak leafed floor—
  in that you were the perfect huntsman.

  Ridiculous—that my heart
still beats harder though I know how
    the story goes, how
killing is a necessity in some circumstances, when
  need demands, or a silvered mirror.

Open my chest and the heart falls out—
  wipe it clean of twig and leaf.
It's no shame that you can't say
  no. You always loved older women.

Glistening, my heart
    bleats through fogging cellophane—
      even that is alright.

Omit the details. Tell instead how you couldn't—
  found a deer and slew it,
took that heart to the
  hungry queen. I don't mind.
    Envoy is both messenger and message,
    envy a cousin to need.

[*The World—stands—solemner—to me*]

The wind was a man who carried me
high over the world in his elbow crook.

Eggshell, he called me, *fingernail girl*,
wrapping me tight in his breast pocket,

or letting me tug his feathery mustache,
rein tight his gray head. I was the finest

lady with an acorn cup, and my retinue
danced, the ants

swept their feelers as
they curtsied, the crickets sawed

a tromping tune. I thought he meant—
not perfect—but a house nestled

downstream of any turbulence,
soft murmurs in my ear at night.

Swallow my tears, he'd say,
or drown. I did my part—I was

laced with salt in every crevice.
Even my fingers, sad.

Maudlin tunes,
no more bawdy scraping jigs, and

ere I knew it, my belly took on a hunger,
rumbling with a child that once born,

took all the wind from the world,
opening up its lungs once, twice, to yell—

my god, the sound—then fluttered
empty, and we never breathed again.

[*Recollect the Face of me*]

Remember me as an
elephant figurine,
chipped trunk, one ear,
or a tailless squirrel
languishing in dust.
Let me be that
ever-vexing, ever-present something,
cast away, retrieved.

Today I will be a porcelain
table for a one-legged doll,
her black sculpted hair scratched,
eyes fixed ahead.

For you I festoon
a spread of china bits, tea
cups, plastic fish.
Every detail of our life
observed in miniature—there is your
folded napkin, your
match and cigarette,
elegant, elegant.

[*Where Thou art—that—is home—*]

What about the explorers? I forgot
how they ended up. They were islanded,
etc., and she tried to
refresh him with her cool body,
elegy his life before her.

The man attempted a radio from coconut
husks. He built a raft
of flotage, and every night she
untied its knots. *This will never—*
again, it breaks—and she could not
restrain a smile.

This is something I've heard,
that a woman's strength is trickery,
hard-and-fast. I can't remember
all she did. She Circed as she could,
turned all visitors to swine,
inspired water to wine.
She's not a monster.
Had he ever loved her, what then?
Of the softest fabric she
made a shroud he could have carried,
even in his pocket.

[I dreaded that first Robin, so]

In snow, I was redundant,
                              dimple to the blank plain.
Raccoons circled me wide. The deer shied,
          every one. I was alone, but

a trained bear cultivates some love of its bells, and I
                                        danced, too—
editing my body to partner singular—

          this precision
holds the leg when the will fails—I forgot
                all his forgots, and was

the clean thing once more. But the earth
forgot me, too, and kept turning, and spring

          insinuated so much—the little creek swelled,
rushes pricked out, and everywhere daffodils
          swished their skirts, just like he said
they would. My gown, once so crystal,

          rolled down my body in fat tears, leaving me
obvious.   *Hold still*, I cried, but the robin's
                              breast blared so red—

it's a familar sting, memory,
          new blooming to full blown—his face

shuffling before my eyes again,
          forgetting my forgetting his forgot.

2. THE WORLD LIKE A WORLD LIKE A WORLD

[*This heart that broke so long*]

The hound leaps down from the moon. You are the hare,
        heaving your ropy muscles across the forest floor.
                Indolent once in your lovely white, lazing under
swags of offerings, blossoms, fruit. Now running
        hurly-burly   tumult and scrabbling back paws,
eating only in furtive bolts and the whites
        always showing. You were a girl, but no more;

remembrance makes the rabbit rabbit faster
        to the hound that courses the track. The meat
tastes sweet as gumdrops. The girl you were
                had a little dog she fed from her plate when
able. That dog is old now, probably dead.

        This one needs a collar. This one has been
bred to jet sheen, frictionless alacrity.
                Running though its pads tear, though its lungs burst.

O the hound loves the hare. Loves the hare's
        kerning path and how its feet scrabble for purchase,
emdashing across the page. That's you, the white
                space stretching further and further, arcing
over rivers, over paragraphs and epistles, desperately

        lunging for a safe margin, a burrow to comma into,
or a tunnel bracketed. The hound loves the girl
                not the hare but the hare will do and you
girl it faster and your hair streams uninterrupted.

[To my small Hearth His fire came—]

The sea took the house back, floor by floor,
          opened the doors,
     my mother's rooms, devoured by a rushing
              yawn of blankness,

so too my father's books, yellowed
           mythologies, and his father's,
     and my name, barely
legible, inside his Oxford Shakespeare.
Long ago this happened.

How else to explain the constant
     echo when I climb the last stair?
A collapsed vacuum. The air
          rushed in. The door
    to the attic
        has not opened for years—
has it? With the roof thrown open,

    it's colder, and there is little to burn.
Some coupons she clipped
        for the sake of clipping, some records
    I could hear but not touch—

rapid spark,
    eager flame in my hand, I

carry on though the sea has
    a shell to put me in, my father,
my mother, a spoonful
    each to drown me.

[*Hope is a strange invention*—]

Half a slice, then a whole moon,
orbits down my throat to dissolve my fears,
       psalm of modern medicine that scrubs me
         elegant and cool, lays a chill hand to my forehead.
It's my mother's, or her
                  shadow, vague
                  against my bedroom wall.

Somewhere down the street, a woman laughs,
       the bass rises and falls, a hymn to bravado that
          riffs on sex. This is

after childhood.   After a shadow fell across my true
                 name, and a fairy
gave me a new one. He called me Muckwit, Steamface,
Eyeseep.   I slept under the hill and covered my face
      in crystal lacewings, rubbed my skin in pig shit.
        Name me worse. I closed my eyes for his kiss,
vaccine to happiness, or worse, bliss.

Even after the prince tugged me from the ground,
      named me *Darling*, called me *Dear*, I wanted
to cram my body into rabbit warrens, fox dens,
      I wanted the sadness of rotting fruit,
         of knowing my place and staying,
not these white pills laced with sun.

[*The Robin is the One*]

The childhood I remember
                has never happened,
        elided as it is.

Rather than correct it, I
        obscure long stretches,
bowdlerizing in particular
        instances of passion in my
        nascent adolescence.

It's how I can pretend away
                such a common beginning,
        tidy up the messy house I lived in,
                home it into something
        easy listening and gentle,
                obliterate the walls that hid
nothing of my parents' rages.
                Erase the boys I kissed before you.

[*Experiment to me*]

East of me—what I call *left*—I saw the lines
       x'd out, then reinscribed. To the west,

paper without imprint, a pool of cream.
       East of me you wrote me,   then unwrote me.
Right of me I disappeared. What a woman

      I am, nudged out by a strikethrough,
mistake, mistake. Once, I leaned—

      evening falling like ash—
naked against the picture window,

the lights inside all lit, listing like
      torches, so that all the neighbors could
observe my honesty. To my right,

my reflection gazing back—no pity there—
east of me, the burnished sky.

[He forgot—and I—remembered—]

Honest-to-God is hardly—everyone lies,
        especially when they need a celestial
                finger on their slippery knot. Lord,
                        O so big and shiny, please please
        regard me just a little, remember how
                good I was just last month, before that bit
        of slippage with the New Year?
That girl in accounting whose
        ass gives me such a joyful feeling—even
now, months later, I can't help but
                draw my eyes to it as she walks by.
        It's like a hymn to my own weakness,
                raucous and triumphant.   Forget that,
                        except for my repentance. Lord,
make of me an apostle, a good one,
        except maybe not one that does
                much. I want to be the guy that points
        beatifically at your miracles, who says,
"Everyone, look, that guy is walking
right on the ocean!" And
        everyone *would* look, and I'd never
                deny you, or give away the illusion.

[*Departed—to the Judgment—*]

Darling savage, goodbye—I'm off to outer space.
            Even now my space car revs its engine,
propulsion unit standing by—

and while I say my
        regrets—which are many—my love
told, your indifference—in my heart I'm already

eating vacuum packed
        delight, across from my lovely space wife.

Tell your descendants that I visited your planet
        on a fact finding mission, and if I crossed some
tribal boundary—

happily, you are ignorant.
        Even space men
jump too high in low gravity.

        Until you
                desire me, there
        go I, brave and solitary among weaker lights,
my face upturned to the constant constellation.

Earth is a fond memory and your face
near mine—   return to your people.
Tell them of the lonely man, his gleaming rocket!

[*Their Height in Heaven comforts not—*]

This is the cheap pathos of Lost Dog
      (has you seen my dog? Runs not good. Foams.).

Excise Lost Dog, and insert my gray hairs
      in the morning (has you seem agog?
Runs unshod home.).

Heaven has a place, even for me,
      excluded from the glowering host.
In my hand a flaming sward,
golf cart my chariot,
      halleluiah
          trumpet,
          in tinny tiny key,
          no mute.

Heavy the sadness
      each wads into his sock-balled heart—
all are wounded in
             vision, X'd out
eyes, drunk or dead.

Now we are
      close to the sadness
          of a mockingbird waiting, its
mate snared in lime or sodden, still on gutter's edge—
      For how long, Whitman, are we to sing,
          over what ocean?

Remember those gray hairs,
      tenacious and wiry, that
          she in the mirror grown older?

Not I. I has not seen her.
    Or her dog,
        trailing arabesque spume.

[*Candor—my tepid friend—*]

Colorless princess with conical hat,
assemble your ensemble to the virginal standard—

      now comes the unicorn's horn, the antidote to unblushing
dreams, to part your cardigan set,
      obdurate as it's been, to reveal the ivory
ribcage, the collarbone
      meek like a
            yawn.

      The danger is still
      encamped on the edge of the tapestry,
pikes at the ready and led by a threadbare king, but

      in the woods, you could unknot the undergrowth,
          dart your undergarments with green
floss, pink your mouth and cheek—
roam to the edge of the embroidery.
      It's not undressing, it's redressing.

Even the unicorn is tepid.
      Now—
          darn the border tight.

[*There is a Shame of Nobleness*—]

Tear down the house, tear down the
        horizon,
           empty the heavens of stars
row by row, folding them against
           eastern light, and sorting them away.

If with a hammer to the sky's baseboard,
      struggling against earth that won't peel back,

and if with an editing hand,
      suffering is revealed as my sole talent—
         haven't I dismantled enough?

Alone, I scatter folded stars,
myself one more light among them.

     Eyes adjust, the aperture
opens, and we all hum in the chorus
      for a tune neither requiem nor pastoral.
Now I am their own sullen child,
        only sleeping
between songs,
        laced with glow I sing
eyes like cups of light, light like linens
          nothing in the world
            enfolding me—and it feels like

someone plucking at my corners,   drawing me up,
someone folding me into a square,   someone laying me down.

[*Of Bronze—and Blaze—*]

Of universe I know book's breadth,
        fissured by design or accident, cleanly
broken down the spine. Something
                resembling sorry sews it tight.

Orchestra I call it—hope it so—
                nth chair,
Zeppo to the other Marxes.

Elan carries me through the bride,
        allowing for a march's turbulence.

Notice also this influx of the marital
                        domestica, the trappings of huswifery
blinging from my skirts. No guiding hand

lines my pockets or stitched them shut.

Allowing for the universe, I designed
        zillions of these accidents to litter
each path I might take, tripping forward.

[*A narrow Fellow in the Grass*]

At last, the reader asks for parlay,
              no promises,   but kindly requests that the girl
       across these pages at least pause in her
              runnings to listen, listen—*we just want you*
reasonable—and that is no imprisonment.

      Only she's already slipped from the parlor,
waist deep now in Queen Anne's Lace, in
            fluttering monarch butterflies—of course
every butterfly *flutters*—how lazy—She's
      lilting across the field—no–bolting,
         lanky crashing over the fence   and gashing
open a leg, but still running—   Dear Reader,

why do you hound her—   and there's the river
     in which she always drowns, because you
         need her to, you hold her down, and she
     transforms to a snake, to a burning coal, a
hot poker—and you just hold tighter,

         even tighter, until the tiny bubbles
   giggle from her nose, the greater spasms
      rattle her frame and the water carries the death
away, cleans it up and you can always
       say she slipped—why wouldn't she just
         sit—the girl had it coming for going so fast.

[*The Devil—had he fidelity*]

That nibble—me, the mouse—

house or door, I am for all
                    environs. I teacup. I church.

                         Devil to your decorum,
eek! and catch catch,
very me as center of the kitchenverse,

in hole I flee, followed by cartoon cat,
                    low to the ground, scurry scurr.

        He's the big and gray, but
ah, I am the clever.

Devil devil, pull tail—
        his decorum I devour.

Eek eek, says the lady. Only her legs
                         fill the screen, and
        I smile at the infants at home,

dreaming of walking on two legs,
emulating my tail and swagger—

let them learn desire,
if that's what they need,
        to topple the big gray and seize,

yes, the biggest gold cheese.

[*The power to be true to You*]

True to form, if yours I am, and
        heaving to the shore—I practice
exits on this world—

please forgive this
        obvious coffin I'm sailing
        white capped, storm cracked—me—
ever-so-snug in the closed cell foam.

Regard instead how I circle
        to the same place I began,
odding myself from fellow man,
        belly empty on the dark
edged water. My course is plotted more

to your form than fixed by
        ruddy stars. The boat
            untied, drifts. The love poem
every sailor scratches onto skin,
        time blurs into a dancing hula girl.

On shore, there are skyscrapers, ambition
        yawing to the sky. I'm not a man for that.

On a latitude unvarying, I sail to you
        under the moon that slaves me.

[*Herein a Blossom lies—*]

Heart—mine—I haven't addressed you—
even now, I'd hoped I might
          rustle by. You are
ever bossy, fickle in your motion—

in, out—   this is blood, but
                    not my own. Or how can I
account for such redness when I would
          blush only cool indifference?

Loss isn't losing, and you've
          only had such defeats as befits
schoolgirls' weaker vessels.

Shy to warm,
obstinate—it's been years and you still
                         mope for lips unkissed or roses
lining a bed—rot like that. Listen up,

ingrate—from here on out it's
          every beat accounted for—no more
slip ups, no more skips.

[*The Birds Begun at Four o'clock—*]

This is not the dark wood, or the midway
           ha-ha stumbled over. The birds
     eke out a song over the din of leaf
             blowers.
      Into the
          roar they cry
    domain, display their best
           sex-me plumage. Un-
  burdened by indecision, there are no
      Eleusinian mysteries—I'll always
go to the underworld rather than
    undergo this world much further.

      No, nothing dramatic—I mean
  all this in gesture—the dark,
     tall, and lordly—that's who I
fob myself off for. All these

orioles can give it up because when I
    untie my heel's strap and
reveal myself in the glory
    of my shabby bedroom—such a
       cacophony of secondary sexual characteristics.
          Later I will rise to Spring's
   oboe tones, and reborn, shower all who
call love to the unlistening air, with
    kisses of the most exquisite insincerity.

[*Put up my lute!*]

Passing bell—what care I—
        unless you do, passim—refer me,
                tolling through this passional,
        unto the martyr sweet, who,
pressing his ear against the page,
        marks time by the arrows.

Yester crossed me twice,
        left me nocked and ready.

Untie his hands, drag down
        the post—these bells damn—
east I am heading, singing.

[*If those I loved were lost*]

If my mouth would open, such delights
forthcoming—a red balloon inflating,

two doves that coo *Adieu, Adieu*, a rabbit
hatless but polite, a dignified parade of frogs,

otters roiling in a flowing carpet—
slippery, all of it, most untrue but better for

each misprision. I say the word is *dark*, but
I mean *world*, and by dark I meant

let go—it hurts, this pressure, how my arms bruise
over and then bloom pink and clear again.

Very the pain, or verify—either way,
eyes see things differently afterwards,

drowning seems drawing, death made dearth,
while homophones destroy me. You turn

ergo U-turn and terns cartwheel above, such
racket. What do I love—what's lost, the words

etched onto the window pane,
lucid in the breath, but gone again

once warmth recedes. I hang on to facsimile,
slim volumes stacked to form a ladder

to poetry—wait, I meant poverty.

3. THE GLOW OF THE BIG CORRECTION

[Bloom upon the Mountain—stated—]

By my sidelong glance, by my hand's
      linger—I told you my history,
            of rushing home before cock crow,
            of my dancing shoes worn through,
            my petticoat askew.

Untied from
      propriety, I shimmied
over rivers,
      no fear of drowning—

this is how a lost thing
heaps fortune over her like leaves,
eats her way out of a tower of cakes—

my hair grew as long as needed,
      or I cut it loose and spun a coat,
under which I passed as a youth,
new to the world and unstubbled,
      the one who delighted the bored,
                  amorous duke.

It isn't that I loved him, but
             no one else presented.

Sincere apologies for this wayward
         tale, this hand that travels
            along your breeches.
The shy of me is buried in a crystal box,
      evidenced by this hole I carry
dangling from my wrist.

[*He is alive, this morning*—]

Hushed footsteps—this is fresh snow—new to me, to the world,
        even the streetlights lose their buzz, and cone the street, silent.
Insulated against cold, against sound, I am zipped
                                        secure in my downy coat,
and I can barely feel your hand on my back,
        lightly touching, ready to catch me if I slip.

I am new to love, to the world,
                vain in the glory of it—

even the snow is for us,
                the quiet streets at three A.M., the
hum in my head from vodka, from a party

        in which no one (everyone) knew we were,
secretly, fucking—and do you know, in this

moment, that I have already decided,
                or as much as I can, stumbling,
resigned myself, *If this doesn't work, I quit*,
                not knowing if I mean love, or life, or or.

It's New Year's or it's
                new, the year is unspooling, and history
grasps us tighter, this small part.

[I had some things that I called mine—]

Into the garden I ran, crushing snails under my shell-flecked feet,
    happy. All the rabbits shivered
        as I passed. The gate bowed down to greet me.

    Dominion a dress
              suit so I slipped from those stitches.
    On me it looked like mastery,
mastery like a hand to lick,
        ending in a cuff.

      Then free and briefly lit inside,
    het up and burning higher—

      I grieved you with my wanderings.

No fence you made could keep me.
        Glistering morning-glories
            shaking out canticles of pollen,
    touched me, then retreated.

    Allow me to admit—
              these flames that paper my
    interior, like the fur that marks me monster,
          cage me in this shape
    and all I see, until I am little more than a
             Latin caption.

And the wild in me names this
    longing, the love in me destruction—
love a taming I pull against,
        every longing a play for a cage.

Darling, I'll slip into a collar so long as your
           mouth kisses the latch—

In the garden, a god walks, assigning
names, the story of blame, he calls out
                                        Eve.

[*The Merchant of the Picturesque*]

This is pretty, pretty your sleeping body,
      hair shocked out against the pillow,
eyes closed, lashes like a girl's.

Men in sleep aren't boys, but aren't
      exactly men, either—   they soften,
         revert to animal,
            curled-up beast.

Hair shocked out against the pillow,
      arms indifferent to my space.

Not without violence, even now,
      your hands clasp when brushed,
or seek out my haunch, my wrist, and hold

      for a time, release with a soft grunt, affirm
that I'm here, or someone is.

How pretty, your face at rest,
      even soft, how pretty your mouth,
         partly open.
I ask you,
      curled-up beast, with broad back that blocks
         the light,
unlettered, uncouth for the moment, just

      remember, I am a little thing that lies beside,
         eyes open, watching you
      sleeping the sleep of the great backed beast,
quick to stroke your flank, to soothe when
         ugly dreams threaten, to keep
even your thoughts pretty, pretty your hair shocked out against the pillow.

[*Some—Work for Immortality*—]

Slip my letters—nothing convinces.
      Ordinary tongue, everyday use.

          Mister, fold them backwards,
envelope, return to sender,
      words dissolving, ink
orphaned; de-lineate the paper,

      return to pulp, to timber, till living branches
          kiss the horizon. There, it is undone.
For you, I am also unbuttoned all
          over, and stepping out of the manila.

Remember
      in Vermeer's painting, the
milkmaid and her pitcher—how x-rays revealed a
map on the kitchen wall, painted
      over?
Realism trumps beauty,

the map too rich for the kitchen,
      and this
letter too poor for these words.

      In the dark folds of the milkmaid's dress, a letter
          tucked and secret: pen
your answer while I've still enough to read by.

[*To pile like Thunder to its close*]

Tomorrow the veil lifts twice,
        once from my face, once from my body.

Pleased these hands to re-
        invite, pleased to meet you—tin heart—
                long goodbyed.

        Enter paper valentine;
line this one in lead.

        I would it last past all bombs' drop,
kiss to sleeping
        eye to blinking; blinking, I
            toss my past

        high, the ribbon
            unties and we are all showered with petals.

Now only one knot binds my
            desire,
            engine to the future.

Regards the bridegroom:
                tall enough to steer by.
        Of this I know.
I slipped my feet into his loafers,

tuxedoed the sinking
        ship, my body
        clipped and bubbling
            loose from the water's skin—

oh, it's time for the band to play
        S.O.S., it's the moment to
eat the future cake.

[The Voice that stands for Floods to me]

The bride is two part
        hydrogen, one oxygen: burning and breathing, un-
                        evenly yoked—
very very her hair, spun ribbons
               of sugar, varied her bridesmaids
                     impatiently waiting,
carrying her train like queen's attendants,
              enduring the humiliating
taffeta scroop.

Her steps slow
        and measured to the music.
The music
        slow and measured because

             the bride is an *uncut blossom.*
               and therefore trembling
        naif, inclined to the existential:

Do I do, and
              so knot myself in contract?
forgetting the foregone of the caterers' deposit.

        Of a holy subject today we
           roofbeam our gaze,
     rah rah as the appointed holy

lets loose the vows,

       O, my spouse, thy lips drop as the honeycomb (louder)

O beloved,
draw her down to the shore's edge, to the waves never
        sated, where
    the tide pulls at the sand like
        orchestra, where her garment descends in one

    movement like honey,
eager and slow is the sweetness.

[*To Love thee Year by Year*—]

They call it sacrifice—   imagine me a tiny poppy
      on a field of green felt—brief blip of color,

          limitless expanse. I've never felt foreign,
or like a lash in his eye. If it's not love, it's

          very like. Most days it feels the same—
     exacting—he tweezes the stray

thoughts from my speech, cleans up my
      heart with a tortoiseshell comb.
Every lady should have such a man,
      edging her lawn with a sharp rotary blade.

          Year by year—let's call it always—
    editor and editrix. Engaged
         against a flurry of typos, showered in

revisionist white out. I erase his crow's feet,
      buff away his frown. My head—he
yawns it open, scoops out dark foam,
      yesses I've regretted, the tiny poppy
everyone sees flapping to pieces—

And so, we are growing taller, sweeter,
ratified in the glow of the big correction.

[*A Light exists in Spring*]

Animal, vegetable, mineral,
        loosen the category till
                        I fit—

Gloomy with or without raincoat,
                happy in others' un-,
                        tolerant of
        excrement, satisfied with lies—

Xanex, if I could Xerox
        it to double dose—perhaps that would
                shield me from this anxiety.

That's his hand in mine,
        soft animal, hard mineral against
        insurmountable odds—so the novels
nag me to believe, so the movies
slur against my eyelids: Just
        pray to love and all will be well.
Repeat tenfold, twenty.

In country songs,
no one ends happily, but it sounds
gorgeous, it sounds like love, like banjo.

[*You cannot make Remembrance grow*]

Your apartment, emptied out of jade trees,
     of your books and their hidden origami turtles,
         under the couch a copy of WCW, only no more
     couch, and the floor lamp unscrewed
         and left outside for scavengers:

     now it is a room again.

     Now our footprints are massaged
         out of the carpet, and the blinds are raised
           to the drainage ditch.

My darling, the geese that woke us
        at all hours will still
    kiss down to
          end a journey's leg by perching,
           right leg raised, on the arm of a drowned wheelchair.

     Even the woman upstairs—
         mother to the gently retarded boy—
    even she will continue
         marking winter
           by burning down her kitchen, once more.

Remember how your steps home quickened
     as the first fire truck passed, another,
next, you broke into a run through sirens,
clouds of smoke, and officers, to find me
     entire and unharmed,
groggy on the lawn,
     roused from sleep by a fireman.
Oh, someone else will sleep there now, and
wake to the claxon of bird or flame.

[*Such are the inlets of the mind*—]

So this is the *happy* I've heard so much about.
     Under the streetlights the children hear their names
called and dissolve to separate doors.

        Home is where they break you in, and here is that Jack
airing his house of the exponential,
        rolling rat and cat bodies to the curb.

Evening falls drunken, the porches burn their solitary lamps
        to guide the husbands to their rest.

          Happy to be here and wish you—

          end the sentence before
    I cry a tributary. I'll just watch the starlings
nip from tree to tree en masse, shadow cuttings
like a brain's synapses—oak, then pine—October

    eating away at my warmth, my sweater fraying
to thread, then fiber—in film, a dissolve leaves

    some memory before winter arrives—

O I'm leaving bits that the wind takes wide;
        from branch to branch
    the black birds snap,
        half flying, half falling.
Entire cities might light to ruin, in countries
        my tongue can't parse—
I am just this woman,
        nodding. Sweet dreams
    dogs, cats, rats, all.

Notes on Process

On my 29th birthday, I began a formal experiment with Emily Dickinson's work. I took my copy of *The Complete Works of Emily Dickinson* and selected the first line of every 29th poem. These lines became the source of my acrostic poems, which I see as a conversation with her and her work.